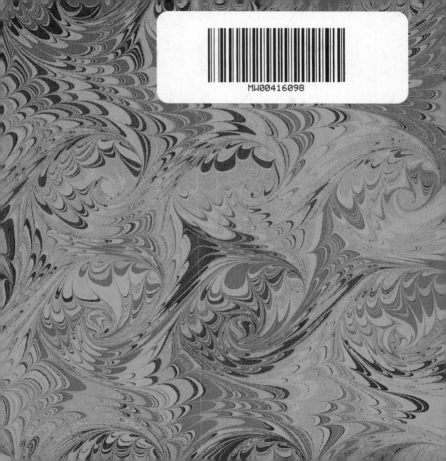

MW00416098

Reflections on Motherhood

· Believing in Ourselves ·

Reflections on Motherhood

Arlene F. Benedict

Ariel Books

·

**Andrews McMeel
Publishing**

Kansas City

Reflections on Motherhood copyright © 1997 by Armand Eisen. All rights reserved. Printed in Singapore. No part of this book may be used or reproduced in any manner whatsoever without written permission except in the case of reprints in the context of reviews. For information, write Andrews McMeel Publishing, an Andrews McMeel Universal company, 4520 Main Street, Kansas City, Missouri 64111.

www.andrewsmcmeel.com

ISBN: 0-8362-2657-7

Contents

Introduction

*W*hat, exactly, is motherhood? It is a lifelong dedication to the growth and well-being of our children: a passion, a job, and a life's work, full of anguish and joy, tears and laughter.

Motherhood challenges and fulfills a woman more than perhaps any other role in life. It can also, however, intimidate even the bravest among us. How can we relax into our role as mother, without worrying about making mistakes? How can we know we're making the right choices for our children?

With quotations and original writings, this book explores these questions and other facets of motherhood. As you read and contemplate each essay, you will probably begin to feel your confidence growing, not only when you internalize a new idea or practice but also when you recognize how many mothering qualities you already have.

What Is a Mother?

A mother is . . . a guardian angel

Infants look to their mothers for everything, for nourishment, comfort, and love. As they grow, however, their increasing need for independence can sometimes lead to conflict, and we, as mothers, can be tempted to react in a controlling "mother-knows-best" manner. While supervision is essential to our children's well-being, we must be careful not to let it become coercive.

Whenever we find ourselves acting as a warden or drill sergeant, we should remember that our role is to guard and guide our children, while still enabling them to reach out and explore the world. We must strike that delicate balance between too much and too little protection. If our children don't venture out on their own, they will never grow; and if they do not develop a strong will and sense of self, they will not thrive.

When we find it difficult to strike the right balance, because we fear for our children's safety, we can envision ourselves as their guardian angel; we can imagine our wings stretched protectively around them; and we can visualize them surrounded by the glow of our love, which guides but does not constrain. Should we find ourselves clamping down too hard on their natural curiosity and sense of adventure, we can work with them to set boundaries, and then accompany them in spirit as they discover the wonders of the world.

Today, I will protect my children while leaving them free to explore and grow.

It's such a powerful connection; it takes me by surprise.
I feel like there's a dotted line connecting me to my son.

—Sarah Langston

•

God could not be everywhere and therefore made mothers.

—Jewish proverb

"You almost died," a nurse told her. But that was nonsense.
Of course she wouldn't have died; she had children.
When you have children, you're obligated to live.

—Anne Tyler

•

There is no influence so powerful as that of the mother.

—Sarah Josepha Hale

I know how the mind rushes back . . .
to infancy, when those stiffened hands were wrapped
around us in twining love; when that bosom was the
pillow of our first sorrows; when those ears . . .
heard our whispered confidence; when those eyes . . .
watched our every motion.

—Caroline Gilman

•

God knows that a mother needs fortitude and courage
and tolerance and flexibility and patience and firmness and
nearly every other brave aspect of the human soul. But because
I happen to be a parent of almost fiercely maternal nature, I
praise *casualness*. It seems to me the rarest of virtues. It is
useful enough when children are small. It is important to
the point of necessity when they are adolescents.

—Phyllis McGinley

$\mathcal{A}$ mother is . . . protector of her children's self-esteem

As children grow, they test themselves against the challenges and standards of the world. Often, they will come up wanting either in their own eyes or in the eyes of others. Often, too, they will find themselves unable to achieve an important goal. At these times, they will need someone to turn to for reassurance; that someone is their mother.

As mothers, we are usually the primary source of support and encouragement for our children; we tell them frequently that they are lovable, smart, talented, and capable. We do this honestly, never telling them what is not true, but helping them to identify their strengths and build on them. We encourage them to develop within themselves a wellspring of confidence and self-assurance.

We make it our primary duty to give them positive reinforcement as frequently as possible. From day one, we are quick with praise and recognition when our children succeed, and we applaud their efforts when they fail. Little by little, our constructive feedback infuses their entire being; with our frequent praise and encouragement, they will develop the confidence and belief in themselves that they will need to become healthy, thriving, and loving adults.

Today, I will help my children build self-confidence by giving them honest praise and hearty encouragement.

The best advice from my mother was a reminder to tell
my children every day: "Remember you are loved."

—Evelyn McCormick

•

Now that I am in my forties, she tells me I'm beautiful . . .
and we have the long, personal, and even remarkably honest phone
calls I always wanted so intensely I forbade myself to imagine
them. . . . With my poems, I finally won even my mother.
The longest wooing of my life.

—Marge Piercy

The little things that I never really noticed all
come back now as I have my own daughter.
Thanks, Mom, for being such a strong model for me.
You made it seem easy.

—Meredith Ralston

•

We want our children to fit in and to stand out.
We rarely address the conflict between these goals.

—Ellen Goodman

It is not until you become a mother that your judgment
slowly turns to compassion and understanding.

—Erma Bombeck

•

A mother understands what a child does not say.

—Jewish proverb

$\mathcal{A}$ mother is . . . a wellspring of strength

Through all the vicissitudes of family life, a mother appears as a limitless source of strength, wisdom, and support in the eyes of her children. They might wonder where Mom gets her stamina and courage, but they never question it. A mother, however, recognizes that her energy is not limitless and that she must find ways to renew herself and her strength in order to meet the challenges that each new day with children brings.

When we become mothers, we make a vow to provide safe harbor for our children. This is no easy task; we are not superwomen and many, if not most of us, have commitments to jobs, friends, and other, perhaps older, family members as well. To be successful at our mothering tasks, we must not be reluctant to seek strength and guidance—even help when necessary—from others, whether it's our friends, our parents, our siblings, or members of our church or synagogue.

We can also seek renewal and guidance through meditation and prayer. When we feel that our stores of patience and forgiveness are depleted, we can pray for help and strength, or simply sit and relax, and let the cares of the day dissipate as our minds become filled with a calming emptiness.

Then, to complete the circle, we can share with our children the lessons we have learned from turning to others so that they, too, will know how to seek support and strength throughout their lives.

Today, if I feel overwhelmed, I will seek solace and strength from others.

In the beginning there was my mother.
A shape. A shape and a force, standing in the light.
You could see her energy; it was visible in the air.
Against any background she stood out. . . .

—Marilyn Krysl

•

I know how to do anything—
I'm a mom.

—Roseanne

My mother's hands are cool and fair,
They can do anything.
Delicate mercies hide them there
Like flowers in the spring.

—Anna Hempstead Branch

•

Sometimes the strength of motherhood
is greater than natural laws.

—Barbara Kingsolver

She had found that the more the child demanded of her, the more she had to give. Strength came up in waves that had their source in a sea of calm and unconquerable devotion. The child's holy trust made her open her eyes, and she took stock of herself and found that everything was all right, and that she could meet what challenges arose and meet them well, and that she had nothing to apologize for— on the contrary, she had every reason to rejoice.

—Maeve Brennan

•

But the actual power a woman has is to make a group of people happy and make them grow in the right way and contribute to the world. Knowing that you release your family in the morning into the day with your love and with your warmth is the richness of life.

—Maria Schell

$\mathcal{A}$ mother is . . . a lifelong friend

Throughout our children's lives, they will always need a friend to stand by them, no matter what. One of a mother's most important roles is to be that unwavering friend.

As our children grow, we may not always like the stages they go through or the personalities they try on; we may dislike their music and their style sense; we may even disapprove of their friends or their career choices. Yet, throughout the years we must provide them with unconditional love and acceptance, regardless of whether or not we agree with the choices our children make on their journey through life.

Our children need to know that they can come to us for advice and support at any time, and that when they do, we will comfort and console them, encourage and inspire them as best we can. We must not withhold our support simply because we do not agree with their decisions: to do so would be a signal that our love for them depends upon whether or not they meet our approval or expectations, which is not the way of mother love.

The message we want to send our children is that our love is without conditions, without measure—and that it will last a lifetime. If our children know in their hearts that we will always be there for them, they will know as well that they will never be without a loyal and supportive friend.

Today, I will let my children know that they can count on my loyalty and friendship for as long as I live.

Because I feel, that in the Heavens above,
The angels, whispering to one another,
Can find, among their burning terms of love,
None so devotional as that of "Mother,"
Therefore by that dear name I long have called you.

—Edgar Allan Poe

•

Romance fails us—and so do
friendships—but the relationship
of Mother and Child remains
indelible and indestructible—the
strongest bond upon this earth.

—Theodor Reik

Mama! Dearest mama!
I know you are my one true friend.

—Nikolai Gogol

•

I couldn't have a better friend than my mother.
I never had to be afraid to talk to her about anything.

—Lacy J. Dalton

•

My mother's love for me was so great
that I have worked hard to justify it.

—Marc Chagall

Finding Our Way

A mother . . . gives her children love, hugs, and reassurance

"Have you hugged your kids today?" How often we see that question on bumper stickers or in magazines; and how often we feel a twinge of regret when we read it! The message and the twinge both serve to remind us how important affection is to the healthy growth and well-being of our children.

From the time our children are babies, they find reassurance and safety in the warmth and comfort of our arms. They learn that a mother's embrace not only makes them feel secure but also shields them from danger, both real and imaginary. When our children become too big to hold in our arms, we give them hugs. A hug can convey any number of things, such as thanks, apologies, encouragement, caring, or security. Or it can simply say "I love you."

Mothers know that the best way to send our children off, whether it's to school, to scouts, or to the baseball diamond, is with a hug. When a hug is the last impression our children carry out the door each morning, they carry with them the knowledge that they are loved. Even a teenager will accept and return a hug now and then.

A hug starts the day right, and ends it perfectly.

Today, I will hug my children.

I think my life began with waking up
and loving my mother's face.

—George Eliot

•

It's easy to complain about children.
But when we want to express our joy, our
love, the words elude us. The feelings are
almost so sacred they defy speech.

—Joan McIntosh

•

Making the decision to have a child—
it's momentous. It is to decide forever to have
your heart go walking around outside your body.

—Elizabeth Stone

They always looked back before turning the corner,
for their mother was always at the window to nod and smile,
and wave her hand at them. Somehow it seemed as if they
couldn't have got through the day without that, for
whatever their mood might be, the last glimpse of that
motherly face was sure to affect them like sunshine.

—Louisa May Alcott

•

Momma was home. She was the most totally human,
human being that I have ever known; and so very beautiful. . . .
Within our home, she was an abundance of love, discipline,
fun, affection, strength, tenderness, encouragement,
understanding, inspiration, support.

—Leontyne Price

$\mathcal{A}$ mother . . . forgives and seeks forgiveness quickly

During the course of normal family life, we all, at times, lash out at one another or create friction in other ways. When we do, it's important that we reestablish the equilibrium of love and support as quickly as possible.

It is not unusual to disagree with our children, nor is it unusual to have to reprimand them. On the contrary, it is healthy to get things that are upsetting us off our chests, so that they don't fester and create resentments that linger long after the angry words or hurtful situations are past.

As mothers, we must try to bring a spirit of reconciliation to all family squabbles. It may not always be possible to stem the flow of angry words, but we can do our best to soothe the hurt feelings they have caused—and do it before another day passes. When we apologize and ask for forgiveness, and encourage all family members to do the same and do it quickly, we teach our children that remorse, revenge, and recrimination only serve to keep the wounds open and prevent healing.

Today, I will teach my children to apologize quickly and to gracefully accept the apologies of others.

The heart of a mother is a deep abyss at the bottom
of which you will always discover forgiveness.

—Honoré de Balzac

•

It is by forgiving that one is forgiven.

—Mother Teresa

•

My mother had a great deal of trouble with me,
but I think she enjoyed it.

—Mark Twain

You have to love your children unselfishly.
That's hard, but it's the only way.

—Barbara Bush

•

A mother's love and prayers and tears are
seldom lost on even the most wayward child.

—A. E. Davis

A mother keeps . . . her children's feelings in mind when she scolds them

A mother must assume and accept her role as disciplinarian, which can be one of her most difficult tasks. It is not always easy to reconcile this facet of motherhood with our role as caregiver and protector, but we must find a way. And more important, we must find a way that works, a way that allows everyone concerned to maintain a healthy self-respect and an equally wholesome respect for one another.

There are inevitably times when we have to reprimand our children in public, whether for their own sake or for the sake of others. But, we can do it gently, and, if possible, take them aside and express our displeasure in a quiet, non-attention-getting manner. In this way, we can let them know that, though their behavior is unacceptable, we do not attach more importance to a breach of etiquette than we do to their self-esteem.

When we are tempted to upbraid our children in front of others (including siblings), it is a good idea to stop for a moment until we get our anger in check. Our children will learn more from us if neither embarrassment nor humiliation get in the way of the lesson we wish to teach; by treating them with respect and consideration, we will increase their faith in the wisdom we have to impart.

Today, if I scold my children I will do so without humiliating them.

Some are kissing mothers and some are
scolding mothers, but it is love just the same,
and most mothers kiss and scold together.

—Pearl S. Buck

•

A mother is neither cocky, nor proud, because she knows
the school principal may call at any minute to report that her
child has just driven a motorcycle through the gymnasium.

—Mary Kay Blakely

Parents learn a lot from their children about coping with life.

—Muriel Spark

•

The real secret behind motherhood . . . love,
the thing that money can't buy. Show your children that
you really and truly love them.

—Anna Crosby

•

My mother had a slender, small body, but a large heart—
a heart so large that everybody's grief and everybody's joy
found welcome in it, and hospitable accommodation.

—Mark Twain

$\mathcal{A}$ mother . . . always makes time for her children

What our children need most from us is love and attention—yet sometimes we get so caught up in our busy lives that we don't even realize how little time we are actually spending with our kids. We schedule our days and our children's days with little time to spare; we take the kids to skating lessons, to the mall, to after-school sports and dances; we plan vacations, go Christmas shopping, pay bills, and do the myriad other things that full lives entail. It is not until we sit back and think about it that we realize that we haven't really connected—that we haven't spent any private time together.

The best moments are often the ones we don't plan: simple, spontaneous experiences like watching a cartoon together or sharing a secret in the car while doing errands. Great moments frequently occur in the sharing of daily tasks—buying groceries, fixing a meal, helping with homework, walking the dog. Often our jobs require us to spend so much of our time away from home that moments like these are hard to come by. Even so, we owe it to ourselves and to our children to find the time to share our lives.

Today, I will create opportunities to be with my children.

The walks and talks we have with our
two-year-olds in red boots have a great deal to do
with the values they will cherish as adults.

—Edith F. Hunter

•

To talk to a child, to fascinate him, is much
more difficult than to win an electoral victory.
But it is more rewarding.

—Colette

More than in any other human relationship,
overwhelmingly more, motherhood means being
instantly interruptible, responsive, responsible.

—Tillie Olsen

Every little minute matters. . . .
Maybe I feel this way because I waited
so long to have a child.

—Jaclyn Smith

A mother is she who can take the place of all others,
but whose place no one else can take.

—Cardinal Mermillod

•

In the evening, after she has gone to sleep,
I kneel beside the crib and touch her face,
where it is pressed against the slats, with mine.

—Joan Didion

A mother . . . teaches her children to
value their own special gifts

One of a mother's most important goals is to instill her children with self-confidence. No matter what trials or disappointments they experience in life, they can rise above them, if they have faith in themselves.

In this regard, we are wise to remember that our children learn best by example. We must show them how to value themselves, their accomplishments, and their dreams. To do this, we have to pursue our own goals and take visible pride in our own accomplishments. When our children realize that we, too, have dreams—even wild and crazy ones—they won't be timid about sharing their own nor will they fear censure or ridicule for dreaming big.

We must encourage our sons and daughters to discover, explore, and develop their talents to the fullest. Whether their particular gifts are academic, artistic, athletic, or domestic, our children will build more satisfying lives and be more contented adults if they, and we, believe in their own unique talents.

The same holds true for their less tangible gifts. When they are surrounded by conflicting opinions or confusing evidence, we must encourage them to pay attention to their own insights and intuition, and let them see that we trust—and act—on our own.

Today, I will encourage my children to develop their talents and trust their intuition.

In all my efforts to learn to read, my mother shared
fully my ambition and sympathized with me and
aided me in every way she could.

—Booker T. Washington

•

And so our mothers and grandmothers have,
more often than not, anonymously handed on the
creative spark, the seed of the flower they themselves
never hoped to see—or like a sealed letter
they could not plainly read.

—Alice Walker

My mother taught me to walk proud and tall
"as if the world was mine." I remember that line,
and I think it brought me some luck.

—Sophia Loren

•

The mother's heart is the child's schoolroom.

—Henry Ward Beecher

Education is the mental railway,
beginning at birth and running on to eternity.
No hand can lay it in the right direction
but the hand of a mother.

—H. O. Ward

•

It's the little things you do day in and day out that count.
That's the way you teach your children.

—Amanda Pays

$\mathcal{A}$ mother . . . encourages her children to rely on themselves

One of the best things we can teach our children is to take responsibility for themselves, whether it's remembering to feed the cat or balancing the demands of school and a part-time job.

Because we love our children so much, many of us make the mistake of doing too much for them. However, if we do the work they've left undone, our children will probably never become independent, responsible adults and citizens.

One way we can encourage our children to become responsible and independent is to point out to them the satisfactions that come with independence: feelings of pride, greater self-esteem, increased confidence. Requiring our children to take their responsibilities seriously, even if these tasks include no more than setting the table and taking out the garbage, is another way we let our children know, and ultimately appreciate, that we take them seriously. And what child doesn't want to be taken seriously?

Today, I will help my children toward independence by allowing them to do for themselves whatever they are capable of.

Loving a child doesn't mean giving in to all his whims;
to love him is to bring out the best in him,
to teach him to love what is difficult.

—Nadia Boulanger

•

A mother is not a person to lean on but
a person to make leaning unnecessary.

—Dorothy Canfield Fisher

It was my mother who taught us to stand up to our problems, not only in the world around us but in ourselves.

—Dorothy Pitman Hughes

•

By no amount of agile exercising of a wistful imagination could my mother have been called lenient. Generous she was; indulgent, never. Kind, yes; permissive, never. In her world, people she accepted paddled their own canoes, pulled their own weight, put their own shoulders to their own plows and pushed like hell.

—Maya Angelou

When I stopped seeing my mother with the eyes of a child,
I saw the woman who helped me give birth to myself.

—Nancy Friday

•

All I am I owe to my mother.

—George Washington

$\mathcal{A}$ mother . . . believes in her ability to be a good mother

The responsibilities of motherhood may seem overwhelming from time to time. We may wonder if we are doing a good job, or if we are making the right decisions for our children. When times like these are upon us, we must not let doubt and fear incapacitate us.

Parenting is often like being up a creek without a paddle—and without a map. Even if we could predict what might be around the next bend, we would still have no guidebook, no rules for every situation. We have to let love be our guide, and have faith that it will lead us in the right direction.

Perhaps the most important question we can ask ourselves when we are in doubt as to what to do is whether or not the action we plan to take is the one that will, ultimately, increase our child's happiness and well-being. If we can answer "yes" to that question, then we should proceed, and take each step with the confidence that we are doing the best job we possibly can. No mother can do more.

Today, I will be confident that my love is the best compass I can use to direct my children's lives.

Most mothers are instinctive philosophers.

—Harriet Beecher Stowe

•

The more people have studied different methods of
bringing up children the more they have come to the
conclusion that what good mothers and fathers instinctively
feel like doing for their babies is the best after all.

—Benjamin Spock

One good mother is worth a hundred schoolmasters.

—George Herbert

•

My mother told me stories all the time . . .
and in all of those stories she told me who I was,
who I was supposed to be, whom I came from,
and who would follow me. In this way, she taught me
the meaning of the words she said, that all life is a
circle and everything has a place within it.

—Paula Gunn Allen

I had already found that motherhood was a profession by itself,
just like schoolteaching and lecturing, and that once one
was launched on such a career, she owed it to herself to become
as expert as possible in the practice of her profession.

—Ida B. Wells-Barnett

The role of mother is probably the most
important career a woman can have.

—Janet Mary Riley

•

The text of this book
was set in Bembo and Isadora
by Sally McElwain.

•

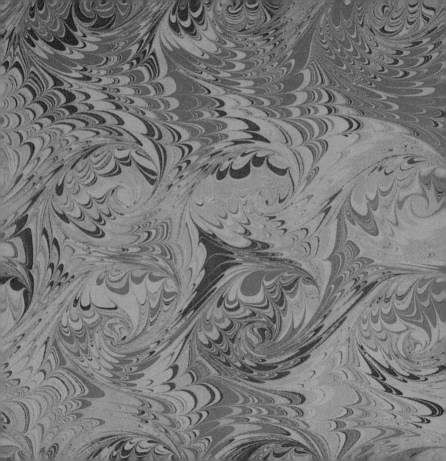